In Between Love & Heartbreak

A collection of poems on Love, Heartbreak & Everything

In-Between

By Rae Williams

Dedication

This book is dedicated to my family, for always encouraging me to write freely or whatever else my heart desired. This book is also dedicated to those who the poems were created for. Thank you for the pain, the bliss, the lessons and the ammunition for me to write. If it were not for you and you and you and you- these words would have never been created. Thank you, sincerely.

Contents

Section 1   Love

Section 2   Heart Aches & Heartbreaks

Section 3   Everything In-between

Section 1
Love

Drunk In Love

His lips meet mine like it is his last breath

But after he breathes me in, he is high.

High off my scent, my cupid bow lips,

My cinnamon strip, sweet licorice honey dip.

All the while we sip, to the timing of my dancing hips-

is he hypnotized by my magic trick?

Is he enjoying this?

We laugh at another notion,

As he continues to drink my potion.

Never questioning my intentions.

Beautiful Love

He treats me like poetry.

Sweet phrases filled with love and flattery.

He takes good care to dot his I's and cross all the T's.

He speaks so sweetly, and always caresses so gently.

If this isn't love, I don't know what could be.

It's almost unbelievable how this man treats me like poetry

I Won't Go

This feeling that you give me gets me

Lifted. I mean, I feel so splendid.

Refuse to let you escape, I get so full of your taste.

This obsession is more than lust, I need you to be mine.

Look me in the eyes and you'll see it's true. I'd hate to be

without you.

Dreaming of You

I dream of sweet melodies and

Your laugh being my symphony.

Of heart beats that make me dance

as if I've heard this song a million times

and the way you strum the drums make me hum

like I know all the words.

Butterflies

There is something so sweet about

kisses to the forehead,

that feel as if my temples are the

resting place for where butterflies tread.

I have dreamt of many beautiful

places, but none as perfect as lying beside

you in bed.

I could talk of being wrapped in

your arms for eternity, but few would

understand-

How it feels to be so vulnerable,

because only a few can.

Body Language

God, I love your body language.

The way it speaks only me, even in

a crowded room of beautiful bodies and charming smiles

your hips always face me.

Your eyes light up when you look into mine and

somehow your protective yet gentle hand finds mine.

Your body language is enthralling, even without your gaze.

It captures me, holds me hostage and I don't think I'll ever look

away.

One Night

It was beautiful, sweet, tempting.

If for but a moment in time,

We were strangers in the night both

searching for the light.

I gave you my hand, you held on tight.

It was perfect for but a moment,

while everything else escaped our minds.

Sunshine

A room full of people,

Yet her eyes never leave you.

Traced steps and visual stimulation

fuel her imagination.

Her eyes dance with excitement at your

sight.

Beams flicker across her temple, sweet

and light.

Shadows cringe at the thought of their

plights, how can the sun still shine in

the deep of night?

Section 2
Heart Aches & Heart Breaks

Pained

Inextricable.

Can anything match this level of pain?

It's no longer March, yet I still feel the rain.

Not quite making sense, but fighting to remain in the game.

Simply because you don't want to lose-

What has already been lost

Tear Drops

When it rains, baby my heart pours.

I remember all we talked about,

how we swore to be so much more.

As the drops hit my window pane

I reminisce on how sweetly you

spoke my name.

Do you remember?

I will never forget the last time.

The taste is stamped on my

buds, chills still run down my spine.

No longer my own, but always

Mine.

A Different World

In a different world, we would

be together.

No longer daydreaming, but planning

forever.

You'd play with my hair, and into your

soul I'd stare.

In a different world.

Such a beautiful phrase, but shattering as well.

Always a gentle reminder that you will never belong to me.

Don't Stay

I welcome you to the ramblings of a

maniac still high off teenage angst,

she welcomes your eyes with temptation

of a taste. But she will leave you thirsty,

feeling unworthy and lying in waste.

And every time she will insist you stay,

but it's better if you go.

Foreshadowed Disappointment

I used to know you.

I almost fell for you.

I would have loved you,

but you'll never know it because

you swear no one sticks around

But now I believe that's how you like it.

Insomnia

Here's to hoping you find refuge in solidarity,

that by chance the walls won't rise higher.

I've found there is foreign hope in clarity,

if only it is not burnt by the fire.

No promises made, so no promise kept.

She lied awake in darkness, while everyone else

slept.

BreakUp

Unveiled masks make for an ugly

conversation-

While you sit in the waiting room

of life, waiting for a transformation.

Tear drops form like condensation on the

outside of a chilled drink you can't wait to drink.

But you've skipped to the end of a brand new beginning.

So where do you go from here?

Harold Square

We held hands at Harold Square,

our fingers intertwined so perfectly.

Your lips met mine, and on sensitive topics

we found they would agree.

The lights shined on only us, baby.

It was clear for everyone to see.

As the air grew brisk, and the night lingered

you pulled me closer and held me tight.

I didn't resist, I could put up no fight.

I miss Harold Square, I miss that night.

Exception

That beautiful smile, with those dimples.

Captivating and full of charm.

I recall your body temperature, so comforting

and warm.

You finished my sentences, as I did yours.

You were certainly mine, but now I wonder…

Was I ever yours?

Drowning

It's the memories that will haunt me,

the absence of what once was.

Or perhaps the ideas of what could

have been.

The rush of tangible emotions, that

slowly turned into slow drips of sorrow and

regret.

Flooded thoughts, questions- no

answers and now I'm drowning.

Luckily, I love to swim.

Broken

Perhaps our differences divide us, or ignorance

derides us...

If I knew which I would stop it.

I'd intertwine your breath with my lungs so that we

are in sync as one. If I could, I would give light

to all the dark places in your heart and pray for

the love to never end after the start. See, I've

thought of chasing galaxies with you, and naming

new moons after that charming smile that you do.

But the whole rotation of my earth was somewhere disrupted,

and now I'm pouring all of my thoughts into a volcano of eruptions.

Do You See What I See?

Sometimes I wish I could show you, you

through my eyes.

I wonder if it would make a difference, or change

how you try.

I'd paint a vivid picture of how your smile lights up my sky,

and how your touch sets my soul on fire.

Would it make a difference? Or would you still say

Goodbye?

Torn

I'm torn somewhere between

completely detached and full of

obsession.

These poetry lines are for you

and your disdained heart.

Perhaps you will find me,

laid out by the oak tree,

basking in the sun.

I will greet you with a smile,

and share my story.

For as long as you listen,

you will have my full attention.

But who cares for attention when I'm after your heart?

Lust Always Expires

I need a love that transcends the

hours of infatuation.

Where his hands gladly get tangled in the curls at the nape of

my neck and I have no fear

of him deciding this isn't what he wants.

I'm needy.

Respect, loyalty

and affection 24/7, 365 days of the

Year.

This generation knows little of

that, so I remain #teamsingle, but

Always hopeful.

Because we all glorify hashtags,

Right?

So much stimulation on the internet

No one can feel your person vibration.

Perhaps Never

Rain drops cascade down her

pillow, where the thoughts of the

mysterious flood her brain.

She is strong.

But no one wants to be alone

forever.

And as the days drive on, she

cannot help but be daunted

by the shallow murmurs of never.

Substantial

She is no weekend lover,

she's a soft alarm on Monday morning.

The kind you smile at instead of

hitting snooze.

She's not the party on Friday night,

but the fire that burns bright on the coldest of nights.

She's no weekend lover, so treating her as such won't work.

She's no weekend lover, she promises her love won't hurt.

Sweetest Anomaly

By nature, she is an anomaly.

Sweet, yet strong.

Her love is like the rushing of waters,

but calm like the resting sea.

She looks at you in amazement,

questioning how you can't see...

That wild hearts like hers were created

specifically, to run free.

Yet, your baby blues captivated for a moment.

A moment gone too soon, sad how bad the sun wants to

spend its nights with the moon.

Break The Glass

The moon stretches across my

window.

Faint, dim…but so alluring.

Quite like the reflection in my mirror.

Insecurities dim the shine,

and manage to separate your heart from mine.

I long to break the glass, but the lacerations from the last time

never healed.

Section 3
Everything In-Between

Rain Drops

Her thoughts are equivalent to rain drops,

heavy but so fluid.

She's the calm in the middle of the storm, but

she always brings the rage just in time.

She may lose the beat, but she maintains the

rhythmic hymn of pentameter and rhyme.

Popularity

The hidden issue is that baby girl confuses likes

with self-esteem. But at the end of the day, the likes don't add up.

So now she's stuck.

Trying to figure out who she needs to suck…

up to, to get the attention she feels she deserves.

Not knowing that we live in a time where men are selfish,

and giving of yourself is likely to leave her helpless.

Helpless and in dismay.

She's beautifully chaotic like a rainbow in color disarray.

She's wondering where the pot of gold is,

Searching high and low. No one ever told her that she was the gold.

So how would she know?

Epiphany

If you don't think I'm the prize, you can never expect to win.

I've settled before, but I won't ever settle again.

You see, you've already lost if you can't recognize the treasures I

hold within.

Inspired

My motivation has always been my nay-sayers,

my heart breakers, my just takers.

They build me up to be stronger than I was before.

They leave me only craving more.

Lioness

See, she is exquisite in her own right.

A go getter by nature, prowling even at night.

She loves deeply, concretely but she is her top

priority.

The manifestation of her power is in her resolve to constantly

move forward.

No. Matter. What.

You see, she doesn't quit because she feels like she's

had enough. She doesn't slow down because she's been hurt.

She uses everything she's got to keep moving forward

so she can reach her final destination.

Where she is going is worth continuing to move forward,

no matter how slow she goes or the obstacles that come her way.

That is her true strength.

Permission

She appears so different,

It leaves everyone questioning.

The truth is, she simply allows herself to

feel the elements.

Right now, the sun is kissing her soul.

The waves are caressing her curves.

And her spirit is happy.

Hide & Seek

She finds beauty in her flaws.

She finds order during the chaos.

She is finding herself, only after losing the self she

thought she knew.

Growth. Progression. Self-Love.

I've found you.

Remembering to Smile

Find someone who is so in love with your smile,

that they will do anything to keep it on your face.

But don't wait to find that person, become that person.

Features

She's got shooting stars in her eyes, and a smile comparable to
sunrise.

She's a whirlwind of emotion, and full of passion.

She's not settling for anything less than what she deserves, for fear
of missing some action.

She's resolved to being her own sunshine, and not taking any shade
to ensure her own satisfaction.

Perception

She doesn't see herself as

beautiful,

That's why she craves for you to

say it.

She doesn't want to be a

Distraction, so she waits for you

to implore her.

She wishes not for games, though

she enjoys plays. She prefers art,

Poetry, summer and the night

sky.

See, she'd want you to be her

moon and her shade in the hot afternoon.

She's strong, so men sometimes

forget to be gentle.

She's just a girl, that's

looking for more.

www.ingramcontent.com/pod-product-compliance
Lightning Source LLC
Chambersburg PA
CBHW061757040426

42447CB00011B/2345